Garde   *Epicurus;*

or

Of Gardening in the Year 1685

P. Lely pinx.   G. Vertue Sculp.

Dominus Gulielmus Temple Eques Baronettus
Ser.mi et Pot.mi Mag. Brittanniæ Regis ad Ord.s Fœd.ti Belgij Legatus
Extr.s et apud Tractatus pacis tam Aquis grani quam Neomagi Legat.s
Mediat.s Ejusdem Ser.mi Regis a Secretioribus Consilijs. 1679 .

Upon the Gardens of Epicurus;

or
Of Gardening in the Year 1685

Sir William Temple

PALLAS EDITIONS

Foreword

We think of Sir William Temple today as a great diplomat and author. His writing, which included the influential essay *Of Ancient and Modern Learning*, and his memoirs and correspondence, reveal him as a writer of balanced prose. His marriage to Dorothy Osborne in 1655 was preceded by their remarkable correspondence, which is both touching and psychologically fascinating. Like the ancients, Temple understood and explored in his writings the mental conflicts experienced by men active in political and diplomatic life. In *Upon the Gardens of Epicurus*, he borrows from Montaigne the story of Heraclitus, who turned away from disputatious public affairs and quit the government of his city to entertain himself playing with the boys in the temple porch. Both writers held public business to be 'the most contrary of all others to that tranquillity of mind, which they esteemed and taught to be the only true felicity of man'.

Temple found his tranquillity of mind in the garden. He was inspired by the example of Epicurus who passed his life wholly in the garden; it was there that he studied, exercised, and taught philosophy. Temple admires certain qualities that were found in that Athenian garden—the sweetness of the air, the greenness of the plants, the pleasure of their scent, and, above all, the sense that only in the garden can a man achieve that exemption from cares and solicitude that promotes the ease of both body and mind. In many ways Temple rewrites Epicurus, creating a patchwork from subjects that concern and interest him. His diplomatic skills (in 1668 he negotiated a triple alliance with Sweden and the Netherlands to check the power of France; and he arranged the marriage of William of Orange to Princess Mary of England in 1677) are revealed in his writing about history, and he is clearly interested in philosophy, especially moral philosophy. His passionate search for calm and health led him to enjoy, almost more than anything else, the cultivation of fruit. He did not grow it just to eat but also for how it looked. Horace Walpole wrote of Temple's passion for fruit,

> For Sir William, it is just to observe that his ideas centred in a fruit garden. He had the honour of giving to his country many delicate fruits, and he thought of little else than the disposing them to the best advantage.

Fruit was almost a fetish for him. The current idea of 'five fruits a day for health' would have appealed to him. He writes in a moralising way about eating good things,

So no part of diet, in any season, is so healthful, so natural and so agreeable to the stomach, as good and well ripened fruits: for this I make the measure of their being good.

We learn a lot of practical knowledge from Temple and envision him in his own pleasure garden at his beloved Moor Park, which lay at the foot of the Surrey Hills on the heaths towards Farnham. He loved the English climate and took a real sensualist's pleasure in the fruits of nature, practically singing hymns to the 'perfume…virtue and perpetual verdure' of the orange tree.

But the most famous and influential aspect of this essay is a throw-away remark towards the end, about Chinese gardens and their mysterious beauty:

their greatest reach of imagination is employed in contriving figures, where the beauty shall be great, and strike the eye, but without any order or disposition of parts that shall be commonly or easily observed

It is to this quality that Temple attributed the word Sharawadgi – his own coinage perhaps, or even just possibly a coinage in Chinese of the syllables Sa-lo kwai-chi, sa-lo signifying 'careless grace' and kwai-chi 'surprising' or 'impressive'.

Having planted the seed of all future gardening in this country, Temple quickly retreated to the comfortable certainties of tradition. Horace Walpole, for one, found this incomprehensible, and mocked Temple for his timidity. But it would be a pity if we were to do the same. Few gardeners have been on such familiar terms with both the practice and the philosophy of their art. We could plan a garden from this essay, being sure to make it an oblong shape, and to include flowers, fruit, shade and water, as well as remembering to water our plane trees with wine! And we can all learn from Temple that true happiness lies in cultivating the garden.

Colin Amery
Director, World Monuments Fund in Britain

The same faculty of reason which gives mankind the great advantage and prerogative over the rest of the creation, seems to make the greatest default of human nature; and subjects it to more troubles, miseries, or at least disquiets of life, than any of its fellow creatures: 'tis this which furnishes us with such variety of passions, and consequently of wants and desires, that none other feels; and these followed by infinite designs and endless pursuits, and improved by that restlessness of thought which is natural to most men, give him a condition of life suitable to that of his birth; so that, as he alone is born crying, he lives complaining and dies disappointed.

Since we cannot escape the pursuit of passions and perplexity of thoughts, which our reason furnishes us, there is no way left but to endeavour all we can, either to subdue or to divert them. This last is the common business of common men, who seek it by all sorts of sports, pleasures, play, or business. But because the two first are of short continuance, soon ending with weariness, or decay of vigour and appetite, the return whereof must be attended before the others can be renewed; and because play grows dull if it be not enlivened with the hopes of gain, the general diversion of mankind seems to be business, or the pursuit of riches in one kind or other; which is an amusement that has this one advantage above all others, that it lasts those men who engage in it to the very ends of their lives; none ever growing too old for the thoughts and desires of increasing his wealth and fortunes, either for himself, his friends, or his posterity.

In the first and most simple ages of each country, the conditions and lives of men seem to have been very near of kin with the rest of the creatures: they lived by the hour, or by the day, and satisfied their appetite with what they could get from the herbs, the fruits, the springs they met with when they were hungry or dry; then, with what fish, fowl, or beasts they could kill, by swiftness or strength, by craft or contrivance, by their hands, or such instruments as wit helped or necessity forced them to invent. When a man had got enough for the day, he laid up the rest for the morrow, and spent one day in labour that he might pass the other at ease; and lured on by the pleasure of this bait, when he was in vigour, and his game fortunate, he would provide for as many days as he could, both for himself and his children, that were too young to seek out for themselves. Then he cast about, how by sowing of grain, and by pasture of the tamer cattle, to provide for the whole year. After this, dividing the lands necessary for these uses, first among children, and then among servants, he reserved to himself a proportion of their gain, either in the native stock, or something equivalent, which brought in the use of money; and where this once came in none was to be satisfied, without having enough for himself and his

family, and all his and their posterity for ever; so
that I know a certain lord who professes to value no
lease, though for an hundred or a thousand years,
nor any estate or possession of land, that is not for
ever and ever.

From such small beginnings have grown such vast
and extravagant designs of poor mortal men: yet none
could ever answer the naked Indian, why one man
should take pains, and run hazards by sea and land
all his life, that his children might be safe and lazy all
theirs: and the precept of taking no care for tomor-
row, though never minded as impracticable in the
world, seems but to reduce mankind to their natural
and original condition of life. However, by these
ways and degrees, the endless increase of riches
seems to be grown the perpetual and general amusement or business of mankind.

Some few in each country make those higher flights
after honour and power, and to these ends sacrifice
their riches, their labour, their thought, and their
lives; and nothing diverts nor busies men more than
these pursuits, which are usually covered with the
pretences of serving a man's country, and of public
good. But the true service of the public is a business of
so much labour and so much care, that though a good
and wise man may not refuse it, if he be called to it by
his prince or his country, and thinks he can be of more
than vulgar use, yet he will seldom or never seek it, but
leaves it commonly to men who, under the disguise of

public good, pursue their own designs of wealth, power, and such bastard honours as usually attend them, not that which is the true, and only true reward of virtue.

The pursuits of ambition, though not so general, yet are as endless as those of riches, and as extravagant; since none ever yet thought he had power or empire enough: and what prince soever seems to be so great, as to live and reign without any further desires or fears, falls into the life of a private man, and enjoys but those pleasures and entertainments which a great many several degrees of private fortune will allow, and as much as human nature is capable of enjoying.

The pleasures of the senses grow a little more choice and refined; those of imagination are turned upon embellishing the scenes he chooses to live in; ease, conveniency, elegancy, magnificence, are sought in building first, and then in furnishing houses or palaces: the admirable imitations of nature are introduced by pictures, statues, tapestry, and other such achievements of arts. And the most exquisite delights of sense are pursued, in the contrivance and plantation of gardens; which with fruits, flowers, shades, fountains, and the music of birds that frequent such happy places, seem to furnish all the pleasures of the several senses, and with the greatest, or at least the most natural perfections.

Thus the first race of Assyrian kings, after the conquests of Ninus and Semiramis, passed their lives,

till their empire fell to the Medes. Thus the caliphs of
Egypt, till deposed by their Mamelukes. Thus passed
the latter parts of those great lives of Scipio, Lucullus,
Augustus, Diocletian. Thus turned the great thoughts
of Henry II of France, after the end of his wars with
Spain. Thus the present King of Morocco, after having subdued all his competitors, passes his life in a
country villa, gives audience in a grove of orange
trees planted among purling streams. And thus the
King of France, after all the successes of his councils
or arms, and in the mighty elevation of his present
greatness and power, when he gives himself leisure
from such designs or pursuits, passes the softer and
easier parts of his time in country houses and gardens, in building, planting, or adorning the scenes, or
in the common sports and entertainments of such kind
of lives. And those mighty emperors, who contented
not themselves with these pleasures of common
humanity, fell into the frantic or the extravagant;
they pretended to be gods or turned to be devils, as
Caligula and Nero, and too many others known
enough in story.

Whilst mankind is thus generally busied or
amused, that part of them, who have had either the
justice or the luck to pass in common opinion for the
wisest and the best part among them, have followed
another and very different scent; and instead of the
common designs of satisfying their appetites and their
passions, and making endless provisions for both,

they have chosen what they thought a nearer and surer way to the ease and felicity of life, by endeavouring to subdue, or at least to temper their passions, and reduce their appetites to what nature seems only to ask and to need. And this design seems to have brought philosophy into the world, at least that which is termed moral, and appears to have an end not only desirable by every man, which is the ease and happiness of life, but also in some degree suitable to the force and reach of human nature: for as to that part of philosophy which is called natural, I know no end it can have, but that of either busying a man's brains to no purpose, or satisfying the vanity so natural to most men of distinguishing themselves, by some way or other, from those that seem their equals in birth and the common advantages of it; and whether this distinction be made by wealth or power, or appearance of knowledge, which gains esteem and applause in the world, is all a case. More than this, I know no advantage mankind has gained by the progress of natural philosophy, during so many ages it has had vogue in the world, excepting always, and very justly, what we owe to the mathematics, which is in a manner all that seems valuable among the civilised nations, more than those we call barbarous, whether they are so or no, or more so than ourselves.

How ancient this natural philosophy has been in the world is hard to know; for we find frequent mention of ancient philosophers in this kind, among the most

ancient now extant with us. The first who found out
the vanity of it seems to have been Solomon, of which
discovery he has left such admirable strains in
Ecclesiastes. The next was Socrates, who made it the
business of his life to explode it, and introduce that
which we call moral in its place, to busy human minds
to better purpose. And indeed, whoever reads with
thought what these two, and Marcus Antoninus, have
said upon the vanity of all that mortal man can ever
attain to know of nature, in its originals or operations,
may save himself a great deal of pains, and justly con-
clude, that the knowledge of such things is not our
game; and (like the pursuit of a stag by a little spaniel)
may serve to amuse and to weary us, but will never be
hunted down. Yet I think those three I have named
may justly pass for the wisest triumvirate that are left
us upon the records of story or of time.

After Socrates, who left nothing in writing, many
sects of philosophers began to spread in Greece, who
entered boldly upon both parts of natural and moral
philosophy. The first with the greatest disagreement,
and the most eager contention that could be upon the
greatest subjects: as, whether the world were eternal,
or produced at some certain time? Whether, if produced, it was by some eternal mind, and to some end,
or by the fortuitous concourse of atoms, or some par-
ticles of eternal matter? Whether there was one
world, or many? Whether the soul of man was a part
of some ethereal and eternal substance, or was cor-

poreal? Whether, if eternal, it was so before it came into the body, or only after it went out? There were the same contentions about the motions of the heavens, the magnitude of the celestial bodies, the faculties of the mind, and the judgement of the senses. But all the different schemes of nature that have been drawn of old, or of late, by Plato, Aristotle, Epicurus, Descartes, Hobbes, or any other that I know of, seem to agree but in one thing, which is, the want of demonstration or satisfaction to any thinking and unpossessed man; and seem more or less probable one than another, according to the wit and eloquence of the authors and advocates that raise or defend them; like jugglers' tricks, that have more or less appearance of being real, according to the dexterousness and skill of him that plays them; whereas perhaps, if we were capable of knowing truth and nature, these fine schemes would prove like rover shots, some nearer and some further off; but all at great distance from the mark; it may be, none in sight.

Yet, in the midst of these and many other such disputes and contentions in their natural philosophy, they seemed to agree much better in their moral; and, upon their inquiries after the ultimate end of man, which was his happiness, their contentions or differences seemed to be rather in words, than in the sense of their opinions, or in the true meaning of their several authors or masters of their sects: all concluded that happiness was the chief good, and ought to be the ultimate end of man; that as this was the end of wisdom, so wisdom was the way to happiness. The question then was, in what this happiness consisted? The contention grew warmest between the Stoics and Epicureans; the other sects in this point siding in a manner with one or the other of these in their conceptions or expressions. The Stoics would have it to consist in virtue, and the Epicureans in pleasure; yet the most reasonable of the Stoics made the pleasure of virtue to be the greatest happiness; and the best of the Epicureans made the greatest pleasure to consist in virtue; and the difference between these two seems not easily discovered. All agreed, the greatest temper, if not the total subduing of passion, and exercise of reason, to be the state of the greatest felicity: to live without desires or fears, or those perturbations of mind and thought which passions raise: to place true riches in wanting little, rather than in possessing much; and true pleasure in temperance, rather than in satisfying the senses: to live with indifference to the common enjoyments and accidents of life, and with constancy upon the greatest blows of fate or of chance; not to disturb our minds with sad reflections upon what is past, nor with anxious cares or raving hopes about what is to come; neither to disquiet life with the fears of death, nor death with the desires of life; but in both, and in all things else, to follow nature, seem to be the precepts most agreed among them.

Thus reason seems only to have been called in to allay those disorders which itself had raised, to cure its own wounds, and pretends to make us wise no other way than by rendering us insensible. This at least was the profession of many rigid Stoics, who would have had a wise man, not only without any sort of passion, but without any sense of pain, as well as pleasure; and to enjoy himself in the midst of diseases and torments, as well as of health and ease: a principle, in my mind, against common nature and commonsense; and which might have told us in fewer words, or with less circumstance, that a man, to be wise, should not be a man; and this perhaps might have been easy enough to believe, but nothing so hard as the other.

The Epicureans were more intelligible in their notion, and fortunate in their expressions, when they placed a man's happiness in the tranquillity of mind and indolence of body; for while we are composed of both, I doubt both must have a share in the good or ill we feel. As men of several languages say the same things in very different words; so in several ages, countries, constitutions of laws and religion, the same thing seems to be meant by very different expressions: what is called by the Stoics apathy, or dispassion; by the Sceptics indisturbance; by the Molinists quietism; by common men peace of conscience; seems all to mean but great tranquillity of mind, though it be made to proceed from so diverse causes, as human wisdom, innocence of life, or resignation to the will of God. An old usurer had the same notion, when he said, *No man could have peace of conscience, that run out of his estate*; not comprehending what else was meant by that phrase, besides true quiet and content of mind; which, however expressed, is, I suppose, meant by all to be the best account that can be given of the happiness of man, since no man can pretend to be happy without it.

I have often wondered how such sharp and violent invectives came to be made so generally against Epicurus by the ages that followed him, whose admirable wit, felicity of expression, excellence of nature, sweetness of conversation, temperance of life, and constancy of death, made him so beloved by his friends, admired by his scholars, and honoured by the Athenians. But this injustice may be fastened chiefly upon the envy and malignity of the Stoics at first, then upon the mistakes of some gross pretenders to his sect (who took pleasure only to be sensual), and afterwards, upon the piety of the primitive Christians, who esteemed his principles of natural philosophy more opposite to those of our religion, than either the Platonists, the Peripatetics, or Stoics themselves: yet, I confess, I do not know why the account given by Lucretius of the gods, should be thought more impious than that given by Homer, who makes them not only subject to all the weakest passions, but perpetually busy in all the worst or meanest actions of men.

But Epicurus has found so great advocates of his virtue, as well as learning and inventions, that there need no more; and the testimonies of Diogenes Laertius alone seem too sincere and impartial to be disputed, or to want the assistance of modern authors: if all failed, he will be but too well defended by the excellence of so many of his sect in all ages, and especially of those who lived in the compass of one, but the greatest in story, both as to persons and events: I need name no more than Cæsar, Atticus, Mæcenas, Lucretius, Virgil, Horace; all admirable in their several kinds, and perhaps unparalleled in story.

Cæsar, if considered in all lights, may justly challenge the first place in the registers we have of mankind, equal only to himself, and surpassing all others of his nation and his age, in the virtues and excellencies of a statesman, a captain, an orator, an historian; besides all these, a poet, a philosopher, when his leisure allowed him; the greatest man of counsel and of action, of design and execution; the greatest nobleness of birth, of person, and of countenance; the greatest humanity and clemency of nature, in the midst of the greatest provocations, occasions and examples of cruelty and revenge: 'tis true, he overturned the laws and constitutions of his country; yet 'twas after so many others had not only begun, but proceeded very far, to change and violate them; so as in what he did, he seems rather to have prevented others than to have done what he himself designed;

for though his ambition was vast, yet it seems to have
been raised to those heights, rather by the insolence of
his enemies than by his own temper; and that what
was natural to him was only a desire of true glory, and
to acquire it by good actions as well as great, by conquests of barbarous nations, extent of the Roman
Empire; defending at first the liberties of the ple-
beians, opposing the faction that had begun in Sulla
and ended in Pompey: and, in the whole course of his
victories and successes, seeking all occasions of bounty
to his friends, and clemency to his enemies.

Atticus appears to have been one of the wisest and
best of the Romans; learned without pretending, good
without affectation, bountiful without design, a friend
to all men in misfortune, a flatterer to no man in greatness or power, a lover of mankind, and beloved by
them all; and by these virtues and dispositions, he
passed safe and untouched through all the flames of
civil dissensions that ravaged his country the greatest
part of his life; and though he never entered into any
public affairs, or particular factions of his State, yet
he was favoured, honoured, and courted by them all,
from Sulla to Augustus.

Mæcenas was the wisest counsellor, the truest friend,
both of his prince and his country, the best governor of
Rome, the happiest and ablest negotiator, the best
judge of learning and virtue, the choicest in his
friends, and thereby the happiest in his conversation
that has been known in story; and I think, to his con-

duct in civil, and Agrippa's in military affairs, may be truly ascribed all the fortunes and greatness of Augustus, so much celebrated in the world.

For Lucretius, Virgil, and Horace, they deserve, in my opinion, the honour of the greatest philosophers, as well as the best poets of their nation or age. The two first, besides what looks like something more than human in their poetry, were very great naturalists, and admirable in their morals: and Horace, besides the sweetness and elegance of his lyrics, appears in the rest of his writings so great a master of life, and of true sense in the conduct of it, that I know none beyond him. It was no mean strain of his philosophy, to refuse being secretary to Augustus, when so great an emperor so much desired it. But all the different sects of philosophies seem to have agreed in the opinion of a wise man's abstaining from public affairs, which is thought the meaning of Pythagoras's precept, *to abstain from beans*, by which the affairs or public resolutions in Athens were managed. They thought that sort of business too gross and material for the abstracted fineness of their speculations. They esteemed it too sordid and too artificial for the cleanness and simplicity of their manners and lives. They would have no part in the faults of a government; and they knew too well, that the nature and passions of men made them incapable of any that was perfect and good; and therefore thought all the service they could do to the State they lived under, was to mend the lives and manners of particular men that composed it. But where factions were once entered and rooted in a State, they thought it madness for good men to meddle with public affairs; which made them turn their thoughts and entertainments to anything rather than this; and Heraclitus having upon the factions of the citizens quitted the government of his city, and amusing himself to play with the boys in the porch of the temple, asked those who wondered at him, *whether 'twas not better to play with such boys, than govern such men?* But above all, they esteemed public business the most contrary of all others to that tranquillity of mind, which they esteemed and taught to be the only true felicity of man.

For this reason Epicurus passed his life wholly in his gardens; there he studied, there he exercised, there he taught his philosophy; and indeed, no other sort of abode seems to contribute so much to both the tranquillity of mind and indolence of body, which he made his chief ends. The sweetness of air, the pleasantness of smell, the verdure of plants, the cleanness and lightness of food, the exercises of working or walking; but above all, the exemption from cares and solicitude, seem equally to favour and improve both contemplation and health, the enjoyment of sense and imagination, and thereby the quiet and ease both of the body and mind.

Though Epicurus be said to have been the first that had a garden in Athens, whose citizens before him had theirs in their villas or farms without the city; yet the use of gardens seems to have been the most ancient and most general of any sorts of possession among mankind, and to have preceded those of corn or of cattle, as yielding the easier, the pleasanter, and more natural food. As it has been the inclination of kings, and the choice of philosophers, so it has been the common favourite of public and private men; a pleasure of the greatest, and the care of the meanest; and indeed an employment and a possession, for which no man is too high nor too low.

If we believe the Scripture, we must allow that God Almighty esteemed the life of a man in a garden the happiest He could give him, or else He would not have placed Adam in that of Eden; that it was a state of innocence and pleasure; and that the life of husbandry and cities came after the Fall, with guilt and with labour.

Where Paradise was has been much debated, and little agreed; but what sort of place is meant by it may perhaps easier be conjectured. It seems to have been a Persian word, since Xenophon and other Greek authors mention it, as what was much in use and delight among the kings of those eastern countries. Strabo, describing Jericho, says, *Ibi est palmetum, cui immixte sunt, etiam aliæ stirpes hortenses, locus ferax, palmis abundans, spatio stadiorum centum, totus irriguus, ibi est Regia et Balsami Paradisus.* He mentions another place to be *prope Libanum et*

Paradisum. And Alexander is written to have seen Cyrus's tomb in paradise, being a tower not very great, and covered with a shade of trees about it. So that a Paradise among them seems to have been a large space of ground, adorned and beautified with all sorts of trees, both of fruits and of forest, either found there before it was enclosed, or planted after; either cultivated like gardens, for shades and for walks, with fountains or streams, and all sorts of plants usual in the climate, and pleasant to the eye, the smell, or the taste; or else employed, like our Parks, for enclosure and harbour of all sorts of wild beasts, as well as for the pleasure of riding and walking: and so they were of more or less extent, and of different entertainment, according to the several humours of the princes that ordered and enclosed them.

Semiramis is the first we are told of in story, that brought them in use through her empire, and was so fond of them as to make one wherever she built, and in all or most of the provinces she subdued, which are said to have been from Babylon as far as India. The Assyrian kings continued this custom and care, or rather this pleasure, till one of them brought in the use of smaller and more regular gardens: for having married a wife he was fond of, out of one of the provinces, where such paradises or gardens were much in use, and the country lady not well bearing the air or enclosure of the palace in Babylon to which the Assyrian kings used to confine themselves, he made

her gardens, not only within the palaces, but upon
terraces raised with earth, over the arched roofs, and
even upon the top of the highest tower, planted them
with all sorts of fruit trees, as well as other plants and
flowers, the most pleasant of that country; and thereby made at least the most airy gardens, as well as the
most costly, that have been heard of in the world. This
lady may probably have been native of the provinces
of Chasimer, or of Damascus, which have in all times
been the happiest regions for fruits of all the East, by
the excellence of soil, the position of mountains, the
frequency of streams, rather than the advantages of
climate. And 'tis great pity we do not yet see the history of Chasimer, which Monsieur Bernier assured me
he had translated out of Persian, and intended to
publish; and of which he has given such a taste, in his
excellent memoirs of the Mogul's country.

The next gardens we read of, are those of Solomon,
planted with all sorts of fruit trees, and watered with
fountains; and though we have no more particular
description of them, yet we may find, they were the
places where he passed the times of his leisure and
delight, where the houses as well as grounds were
adorned with all that could be of pleasing and elegant,
and were the retreats and entertainments of those
among his wives that he loved the best; and 'tis not
improbable, that the paradises mentioned by Strabo
were planted by this great and wisest king. But the
idea of the garden must be very great, if it answer at

all to that of the gardener, who must have employed a great deal of his care and of his study, as well as of his leisure and thought, in these entertainments, since he writ of all plants, from the cedar to the shrub.

What the gardens of the Hesperides were, we have little or no account, further than the mention of them, and thereby the testimony of their having been in use and request, in such remoteness of place, and antiquity of time.

The garden of Alcinous, described by Homer, seems wholly poetical, and made at the pleasure of the painter; like the rest of the romantic palace in that little barren island of Phœnicia or Corfu. Yet, as all the pieces of this transcendent genius are composed with excellent knowledge, as well as fancy; so they seldom fail of instruction as well as delight, to all that read him. The seat of this garden, joining to the gates of the palace, the compass of the enclosure being four acres, the tall trees of shade, as well as those of fruit, the two fountains, the one for the use of the garden, and the other of the palace, the continual succession of fruits throughout the whole year, are, for aught I know, the best rules or provision that can go towards composing the best gardens; nor is it unlikely, that Homer may have drawn this picture after the life of some he had seen in Ionia, the country and usual abode of this divine poet; and indeed, the region of the most refined pleasures and luxury, as well as invention and wit: for the humour and custom of gardens may have descended earlier into the lower Asia, from Damascus, Assyria, and other parts of the eastern empires, though they seem to have made late entrance and smaller improvement in those of Greece and Rome; at least in no proportion to their other inventions or refinements of pleasure and luxury.

The long and flourishing peace of the two first empires gave earlier rise and growth to learning and civility, and all the consequences of them, in magnificence and elegance of building and gardening, whereas Greece and Rome were almost perpetually engaged in quarrels and wars, either abroad or at home, and so were busy in actions that were done under the sun, rather than those under the shade. These were the entertainments of the softer nations, that fell under the virtue and prowess of the two last empires, which from those conquests brought home mighty increases both of riches and luxury, and so perhaps lost more than they got by the spoils of the East.

There may be another reason for the small advance of gardening in those excellent and more temperate climates, where the air and soil were so apt of themselves to produce the best sorts of fruits, without the necessity of cultivating them by labour and care; whereas the hotter climates, as well as the cold, are forced upon industry and skill, to produce or improve many fruits that grow of themselves in the more temperate regions. However it were, we have very little mention of gardens in old Greece, or in old

Rome, for pleasure or with elegance, nor of much curiousness or care, to introduce the fruits of foreign climates, contenting themselves with those which were native of their own; and these were the vine, the olive, the fig, the pear, and the apple: Cato, as I remember, mentions no more; and their gardens were then but the necessary part of their farms, intended particularly for the cheap and easy food of their hinds or slaves employed in their agriculture, and so were turned chiefly to all the common sorts of plants, herbs, or legumes (as the French call them) proper for common nourishment; and the name of *hortus* is taken to be from *ortus*, because it perpetually furnishes some rise or production of something new in the world.

Lucullus, after the Mithridatic war, first brought cherries from Pontus into Italy, which so generally pleased, and were so easily propagated in all climates, that within the space of about an hundred years, having travelled westward with the Roman conquests, they grew common as far as the Rhine, and passed over into Britain. After the conquest of Africa, Greece, the Lesser Asia, and Syria, were brought into Italy all the sorts of their *Mala*, which we interpret as apples, and might signify no more at first, but were afterwards applied to many other foreign fruits: the apricots, coming from Epire, were called *Mala Epirotica*; peaches from Persia, *Mala Persica*; citrons of Media, *Medica*; pomegranates from Carthage, *Punica*; quinces, *Cathonea*, from a small island in the Grecian seas; their best pears were brought from Alexandria, Numidia, Greece, and Numantia; as appears by their several appellations: their plums, from Armenia, Syria, but chiefly from Damascus. The kinds of these are reckoned in Nero's time to have been near thirty, as well as of figs; and many of them were entertained at Rome with so great applause, and so general vogue, that the great captains, and even consular men, who first brought them over, took pride in giving them their own names (by which they run a great while in Rome) as in memory of some great service or pleasure they had done their country; so that not only laws and battles, but several sorts of apples or *Mala*, and of pears were called Manlian and Claudian, Pompeian and Tiberian; and by several other such noble names.

Thus the fruits of Rome, in about an hundred years, came from countries as far as their conquests had reached; and like learning, architecture, painting, and statuary, made their great advances in Italy, about the Augustan age. What was of most request in their common gardens in Virgil's time, or at least in his youth, may be conjectured by the description of his old Corycian's gardens in the fourth of the Georgics; which begins,

Namque sub Oebaliæ memini me turribus alti❊.

Among flowers, the roses had the first place, especially
a kind which bore twice a year; and none other sorts
are here mentioned besides the narcissus, though the
violet and the lily were very common, and the next in
esteem; especially the *Breve Lilium*, which was the
tuberose. The plants he mentions are the *Apium*,
which though commonly interpreted as parsley, yet
comprehends all sorts of smallage, whereof celery is
one; *Cucumis*, which takes in all sorts of melons, as
well as cucumbers; *Olus*, which is a common word for
all sorts of pot-herbs and legumes; *Verbenas*, which
signifies all kinds of sweet or sacred plants that were
used for adorning the altars; as bays, olive, rose-
mary, myrtle: the *Acanthus* seems to be what we
called *Pericanthe*; but what their *Hederæ* were, that
deserved place in a garden, I cannot guess, unless
they had sorts of ivy unknown to us; nor what his
Vescum Papaver was, since poppies with us are of no
use in eating. The fruits mentioned are only apples,
pears, and plums; for olives, vines, and figs, were
grown to be fruits of their fields, rather than of their
gardens. The shades were the elm, the pine, the lime
tree, and the *Platanus*, or plane tree; whose leaf and
shade, of all others, was the most in request; and,
having been brought out of Persia, was such an incli-

❊ Temple misquotes: 'alti' should be 'arcis'.

nation among the Greeks and Romans, that they usually fed it with wine instead of water; they believed this tree loved that liquor, as well as those that used to drink under its shade; which was a great humour and custom, and perhaps gave rise to the other, by observing the growth of the tree, or largeness of the leaves, where much wine was spilt or left, and thrown upon the roots.

'Tis a great pity that the haste which Virgil seems here to have been in, should have hindered him from entering farther into the account or instructions of gardening, which he said he could have given, and which he seems to have so much esteemed and loved, by that admirable picture of this old man's felicity, which he draws like so great a master, with one stroke of a pencil in those four words:

Regum æquabat opes animis.

That in the midst of these small possessions, upon a few acres of barren ground, yet he equalled all the wealth and opulence of kings, in the ease, content, and freedom of his mind.

I am not satisfied with the common acceptance of the *Mala Aurea* for oranges; nor do I find any passage in the authors of that age, which gives me the opinion, that these were otherwise known to the Romans than as fruits of the eastern climates. I should take their *Mala Aurea* to be rather some kind of apple, so called from the golden colour, as some are amongst us; for otherwise, the orange tree is too noble in the beauty, taste, and smell of its fruit; in the perfume and virtue of its flowers; in the perpetual verdure of its leaves, and in the excellent uses of all, these, both for pleasure and health; not to have deserved any particular mention in the writings of an age and nation so refined and exquisite in all sorts of delicious luxury.

The charming description Virgil makes of the happy apple, must be intended either for the citron, or for some sort of orange growing in Media, which was either so proper to that country as not to grow in any other (as a certain sort of fig was to Damascus), or to have lost its virtue by changing soils, or to have had its effect of curing some sort of poison that was usual in that country, but particular to it: I cannot forbear inserting those few lines out of the second of Virgil's Georgics, not having ever heard anybody else take notice of them.

Media fert tristes succos, tardumque saporem
Fœlicis mali; quo non præsentibus ullum,
Pocula si quando sævœ infecere novercœ,
Auxilium venit, ac membris agit atra venena.
Ipsa ingens arbos, faciemque simillima lauro;
Et si non alios late jactaret odorem,
Laurus erat, folia haud ullis labentia ventis;
Flos apprima tenax: animas et olentia Medi
Ora fovent illo, et senibus medicantur anhelis.

Media brings pois'nous herbs, and the flat taste
Of the bless'd apple, than which ne'er was found
A help more present, when curst step-dames mix
Their mortal cups, to drive the venom out.
'Tis a large tree, and like a bays in hue;
And did it not such odours cast about,
'Twou'd be a bays; the leaves with no winds fall,
The flowers all excel: with these the Medes
Perfume their breaths, and cure old pursy men.

The tree being so like a bay or laurel, the slow or dull taste of the apple, the virtue of it against poison, seems to describe the citron: the perfume of the flowers and virtues of them, to cure ill scents of mouth or breath, or shortness of wind in pursy old men, seem to agree most with the orange: if *flos apprima tenax* mean only the excellence of the flower above all others, it may be intended for the orange; if it signifies the flowers growing most upon the tops of the trees, it may be rather the citron; for I have been so curious as to bring up a citron from a kernel, which at twelve years of age began to flower; and I observed all the flowers to grow upon the top branches of the tree, but to be nothing so high or sweet-scented as the orange. On the other side, I have always heard oranges to pass for a cordial juice, and a great preservative against the plague, which is a sort of venom; so that I know not to which of these we are to ascribe this lovely picture of the happy apple; but I am satisfied by it, that neither

of them was at all common, it at all known in Italy, at
that time, or long after, though the fruit be now so
frequent there in fields (at least in some parts) and
make so common and delicious a part of gardening,
even in these northern climates.

'Tis certain those noble fruits, the citron, the
orange and the lemon, are the native product of those
noble regions, Assyria, Media and Persia; and though
they have been from thence transplanted and propagated in many parts of Europe, yet they have not
arrived at such perfection in beauty, taste or virtue as
in their native soil and climate. This made it generally
observed among the Greeks and Romans, that the
fruits of the East far excelled those of the West. And
several writers had trifled away their time in deducing
the reasons of this difference, from the more benign
or powerful influences of the rising sun. But there is
nothing more evident to any man that has the least
knowledge of the globe, and gives himself leave to
think, than the folly of such wise reasons, since the
regions that are east to us, are west to some others;
and the sun rises alike to all that lie in that same latitude, with the same heat and virtue upon its first
approaches, as well as in its progress. Besides, if the
eastern fruits were the better only for that position of
climate, then those of India should excel those of
Persia; which we do not find by comparing the
accounts of those countries: but Assyria, Media, and
Persia have been ever esteemed, and will be ever

found the true regions of the best and noblest fruits in the world. The reason of it can be no other, than that of an excellent and proper soil, being there extended under the best climate for the production of all sorts of the best fruits; which seems to be from about twenty-five, to about thirty-five degrees of latitude. Now the regions under this climate in the present Persian empire (which comprehends most of the other two, called anciently Assyria and Media) are composed of many provinces full of great and fertile plains, bounded by high mountains, especially to the north; watered naturally with many rivers, and those by art and labour derived into many more and smaller streams, which all conspire to form a country, in all circumstances, the most proper and agreeable for production of the best and noblest fruits. Whereas if we survey the regions of the western world, lying in the same latitude between twenty-five and thirty-five degrees, we shall find them extend either over the Mediterranean Sea, the ocean, or the sandy barren countries of Africa; and that no part of the continent of Europe lies so southward as thirty-five degrees. Which may serve to discover the true genuine reason, why the fruits of the East have been always observed and agreed to transcend those of the West.

In our north-west climates, our gardens are very different from what they were in Greece and Italy, and from what they are now in those regions in Spain or the southern parts of France. And as most general customs in countries grow from the different nature of climates, soils, or situations, and from the necessities or industry they impose, so do these.

In the warmer regions, fruits and flowers of the best sorts are so common, and of so easy production, that they grow in fields, and are not worth the cost of enclosing, or the care of more than ordinary cultivating. On the other side, the great pleasures of those climates are coolness of air, and whatever looks cool even to the eyes, and relieves them from the unpleasant sight of dusty streets, or parched fields. This makes the gardens of those countries to be chiefly valued by largeness of extent (which gives greater play and openness of air), by shade of trees, by frequency of living streams or fountains, by perspectives, by statues, and by pillars and obelisks of stone scattered up and down, which all conspire to make any place look fresh and cool. On the contrary, the more northern climates, as they suffer little by heat, make little provision against it, and are careless of shade, and seldom curious in fountains. Good statues are in the reach of few men, and common ones are generally and justly despised or neglected. But no sorts of good fruits or flowers, being natives of the climates, or usual among us (nor indeed the best sort of plants, herbs, salads for our kitchen gardens themselves); and the best fruits not ripening without the advantage of walls and palisades, by reflection of the faint heat we receive from the sun, our gardens are made of smaller compass, seldom exceeding four, six, or eight acres; enclosed with walls, and laid out in a manner wholly for advantage of fruits, flowers, and the product of kitchen gardens in all sorts of herbs, salads, plants, and legumes, for the common use of tables.

These are usually the gardens of England and Holland, as the first sort are those of Italy, and were so of old. In the more temperate parts of France, and in Brabant (where I take gardening to be at its greatest height), they are composed of both sorts, the extent more spacious than ours; part laid out for flowers, others for fruits; some standards, some against walls or palisades, some for forest trees, and groves for shade, some parts wild, some exact; and fountains much in request among them.

But after so much ramble into ancient times, and remote places, to return home and consider the present way and humour of our gardening in England; which seem to have grown into such vogue, and to have been so mightily improved in three or four and twenty years of his Majesty's reign, that perhaps few countries are before us, either in the elegance of our gardens, or in the number of our plants; and I believe none equals us in the variety of fruits which may be justly called good; and from the earliest cherry and strawberry, to the last apples and pears, may furnish every day of the circling year. For the taste and perfection of what we esteem the best, I may truly say, that the French, who have eaten my peaches and grapes at Sheen, in no very ill year, have generally concluded, that the last are as good as any they have eaten in France, on this side Fontainebleau; and the first as good as any they have eaten in Gascony; I mean those which come from the stone, and are properly called peaches, not those which are hard, and are termed pavies; for these cannot grow in too warm a climate, nor ever be good in a cold; and are better at Madrid, than in Gascony itself. Italians have agreed, my white figs to be as good as any of that sort in Italy, which is the earlier kind of white fig there; for in the latter kind, and the blue, we cannot come near the warm climates, no more than in the Frontignac or Muscat grape.

My orange trees are as large as any I saw when I was young in France, except those of Fontainebleau, or what I have seen since in the Low Countries, except some very old ones of the Prince of Orange's; as laden with flowers as any can well be, as full of fruit as I suffer or desire them, and as well tasted as are commonly brought over, except the best sorts of Seville and Portugal. And thus much I could not but say in defence of our climate, which is so much and so generally decried abroad, by those who never saw it; or, if they have been here, have yet perhaps seen no more of it, than what belongs to inns, or to taverns and ordinaries; who accuse our country for their own defaults, and speak ill, not only of our gardens and

houses, but of our humours, our breeding, our customs and manners of life, by what they have observed
of the meaner and baser sort of mankind; and of company among us, because they wanted themselves, perhaps, either fortune or birth, either quality or merit,
to introduce them among the good.

I must needs add one thing more in favour of our
climate, which I heard the King say, and I thought
new and right, and truly like a King of England, that
loved and esteemed his own country: 'twas in reply to
some of the company that were reviling our climate,
and extolling those of Italy and Spain, or at least of
France: he said, he thought that was the best climate,
where he could be abroad in the air with pleasure, or
at least without trouble or inconvenience, the most
days of the year, and the most hours of the day; and
this he thought he could be in England, more than in
any country he knew of in Europe. And I believe it is
true, not only of the hot and cold, but even among our
neighbours in France, and the Low Countries themselves; where the heats or the colds, and changes of
seasons, are less treatable than they are with us.

The truth is, our climate wants no heat to produce
excellent fruits; and the default of it is only the short
season of our heats or summers, by which many of the
latter are left behind, and imperfect with us. But all
such as are ripe before the end of August, are, for
aught I know, as good with us as anywhere else. This
makes me esteem the true region of gardens in

England, to be the compass of ten miles about London; where the accidental warmth of air, from the fires and steams of so vast a town, makes fruits, as well as corn, a great deal forwarder than in Hampshire or Wiltshire, though more southward by a full degree.

There are, besides the temper of our climate, two things particular to us, that contribute much to the beauty and elegance of our gardens, which are the gravel of our walks, and the fineness and almost perpetual greenness of our turf. The first is not known anywhere else, which leaves all their dry walks, in other countries, very unpleasant and uneasy. The other cannot be found in France or in Holland as we have it, the soil not admitting that fineness of blade in Holland, nor the sun that greenness in France, during most of the summer; nor indeed is it to be found but in the finest of our soils.

Whoever begins a garden, ought in the first place, and above all, to consider the soil, upon which the taste of not only his fruits, but his legumes, and even herbs and salads, will wholly depend; and the default of soil is without remedy: for although all borders of fruit may be made with what earth you please (if you will be at the charge) yet it must be renewed in two or three years, or it runs into the nature of the ground where 'tis brought. Old trees spread their roots further than anybody's care extends, or the forms of the garden will allow; and after all, where the soil about you is ill, the air is so too in a degree, and has influence upon the taste of fruit. What Horace says of the productions of kitchen gardens, under the name of *Caulis*, is true of all the best sorts of fruits, and may determine the choice of soil for all gardens.

Caule suburbano, qui siccus crevit in agris,
Dulcior, irriguis nihil est elutius hortis.

Plants from dry fields those of the town excel,
Nothing more tasteless is than watered grounds.

Any man had better throw away his care and his money upon anything else than upon a garden in wet or moist ground. Peaches and grapes will have no taste but upon a sand or gravel; but the richer these are, the better; and neither salads, peas, or beans, have at all the taste upon a clay or rich earth, as they have upon either of the others, though the size and colour of fruits and plants may, perhaps, be more upon the worse soils.

Next to your choice of soil, is to suit your plants to your ground, since of this everyone is not master; though perhaps Varro's judgement upon this case is the wisest and the best; for to one that asked him, what he should do if his father or ancestors had left him a seat in an ill air, or upon an ill soil? He answered, Why sell it, and buy another in good. But what if I cannot get half the worth? Why then take a quarter; but however sell it for any thing, rather than live upon it.

Of all sorts of soil, the best is that upon a sandy gravel, or a rosiny sand; whoever lies upon either of these may run boldly into all the best sort of peaches and grapes, how shallow soever the turf be upon them; and whatever other tree will thrive in these soils, the fruits shall be of a much finer taste than any other: a richer soil will do well enough for apricots, plums, pears, or figs; but still the more of the sand in your earth the better, and the worse the more of the clay, which is proper for oaks, and no other tree that I know of.

Fruits should be suited to the climate among us, as well as the soil; for there are degrees of one and the other in England, where 'tis to little purpose to plant any of the best fruits; as peaches or grapes, hardly, I doubt, beyond Northamptonshire, at the furthest northwards: and I thought it very prudent in a gentleman of my friends in Staffordshire, who is a great lover of his garden, to pretend no higher, though his soil be good enough, than to the perfection of plums; and in these (by bestowing south walls upon them) he has very well succeeded, which he could never have done in attempts upon peaches and grapes; and a good plum is certainly better than an ill peach.

When I was at Cosevelt, with that Bishop of Munster, that made so much noise in his time, I observed no other trees but cherries in a great garden he had made. He told me the reason was, because he found no other fruit would ripen well in that climate, or upon that soil; and therefore, instead of being curious in others, he had only been so in the sorts of that, whereof he had so many, as never to be without them from May to the end of September.

As to the size of a garden, which will perhaps, in time, grow extravagant among us, I think from four or five to seven or eight acres is as much as any gentleman need design, and will furnish as much of all that is expected from it, as any nobleman will have occasion to use in his family.

In every garden four things are necessary to be provided for, flowers, fruit, shade, and water; and whoever lays out a garden without all these, must not pretend it in any perfection: it ought to lie to the best parts of the house, or to those of the master's commonest use, so as to be but like one of the rooms out of which you step into another. The part of your garden next to your house (besides the walks that go round it) should be a parterre for flowers, or grass-plots bordered with flowers; or if, according to the newest mode, it be cast all into grass-plots and gravel-walks, the dryness of these should be relieved with fountains, and the plainness of those with statues; otherwise, if large, they have an ill effect upon the eye. However, the part next to the house should be open, and no other fruit but upon the walls. If this take up one half of the garden, the other should be fruit trees, unless some grove for shade lie in the middle. If it take up a third part only, then the next third may be dwarf trees, and the last standard fruit; or else the second part fruit trees, and the third all sorts of winter greens, which provide for all seasons of the year.

I will not enter upon any account of flowers, having only pleased myself with seeing or smelling them, and not troubled myself with the care, which is more the ladies' part than the men's; but the success is wholly in the gardener. For fruit, the best we have in England, or I believe can ever hope for, are, of peaches, the white and red Maudlin, the Minion, the Chevreuse, the Ramboullet, the Musk, the Admirable, which is late; all the rest are either varied by names, or not to be named with these, nor worth troubling a garden, in my opinion. Of the pavies, or hard peaches, I know none good here but the Newington, nor will that easily hang till 'tis full ripe. The forward peaches are to be esteemed only because they are early, but should find room in a good garden, at least the white and brown Nutmeg, the Persian, and the violet Musk. The only good nectarines are the Murry and the French; of these there are two sorts, one very round, and the other something long, but the round is the best: of the Murry there are several sorts, but, being all hard, they are seldom well ripened with us.

Of grapes, the best are the Chasselas, which is the better sort of our white muscadine (as the usual name was about Sheen); 'tis called the pearl-grape, and ripens well enough in common years, but not so well as the common black, or currand, which is something a worse grape. The parsley is good, and proper enough to our climate; but all white Frontignacs are difficult, and seldom ripe unless in extraordinary summers.

I have had the honour of bringing over four sorts into England; the Arboyse, from the Franche Comté, which is a small white grape, or rather runs into some small and some great upon the same bunch; it agrees well with our climate, but is very choice in soil, and must have a sharp gravel; it is the most delicious of all grapes that are not muscat. The Burgundy, which is a grizelin or pale red, and of all others is surest to ripen in our climate, so that I have never known them to fail one summer these fifteen years, when all others have; and have had it very good upon an east wall. A black muscat, which is called the Dowager, and ripens as well as the common white grape. And the fourth is the Grizelin Frontignac, being of that colour, and the highest of that taste, and the noblest of all grapes I ever ate in England; but requires the hottest wall and the sharpest gravel; and must be favoured by the summer too, to be very good. All these are, I suppose, by this time pretty common among some gardeners in my neighbourhood, as well as several persons of quality; for I have ever thought all things of this kind, the commoner they are made, the better.

Of figs there are among us the white, the blue, and the tawny: the last is very small, bears ill, and I think but a bauble. Of the blue there are two or three sorts, but little different, one something longer than the other; but that kind which swells most is ever the best. Of the white I know but two sorts, and both excellent, one ripe in the beginning of July, the other in the end of September, and is yellower than the first; but this is hard to be found among us, and difficult to raise, though an excellent fruit.

Of apricots, the best are the common old sort, and the largest Masculin; of which this last is much improved by budding upon a peach stock. I esteem none of this fruit but the Brussel's apricot, which grows a standard, and is one of the best fruits we have; and which I first brought over among us.

The number of good pears, especially summer, is very great, but the best are the Blanquet, Robin, Rousselet, Rosati, Sans, Pepin, Jargonelle. Of the autumn, the Buree, the Vertelongue, and the Bergamot. Of the winter, the Vergoluz, Chasseray, St. Michael, St. Germain, and Ambret. I esteem the Bon-Cretien with us good for nothing but to bake.

Of plums, the best are St. Julian, St. Catharine, white and blue Pedrigon, Queen-mother, Sheen-plum, and Cheston.

Beyond the sorts I have named, none I think need trouble himself, but multiply these rather than make room for more kinds; and I am content to leave this register, having been so often desired it by my friends, upon their designs of gardening.

I need say nothing of apples, being so well known among us; but the best of our climate, and I believe of all others, is the Golden Pippin; and for all sorts of uses: the next is the Kentish pippin; but these I think are as far from their perfection with us as grapes, and yield to those of Normandy, as these to those in Anjou, and even these to those in Gascony. In other fruits the defect of sun is in a great measure supplied by the advantage of walls.

The next care to that of suiting trees with the soil, is that of suiting fruits to the position of walls. Grapes, peaches, and winter pears, to be good, must be planted upon full south, or south-east; figs are best upon south-east, but will do well upon east and south-west: the west are proper for cherries, plums, or apricots; but all of them are improved by a south wall both as to early and taste: north, north-west, or north-east, deserve nothing but greens; these should be divided by woodbines or jessamines between every green, and the other walls by a vine between every fruit tree; the best sorts upon the south walls, the common white and black upon east and west, because the other trees, being many of them (especially peaches) very transitory; some apt to die with hard winters, others to be cut down and make room for new fruits: without this method the walls are left for several years unfurnished; whereas the vines on each side cover the void space in one summer, and when the other trees are grown, make only a pillar between them of two or three feet broad.

Whoever would have the best fruits, in the most perfection our climate will allow, should not only take care of giving them as much sun, but also as much air as he can; no tree, unless dwarf, should be suffered to grow within forty foot of your best walls, but the farther they lie open is still the better. Of all others, this care is most necessary in vines, which are observed abroad to make the best wines, where they lie upon sides of hills, and so most exposed to the air and the wind. The way of pruning them too is best learned from the vineyards, where you see nothing in winter, but what looks like a dead stump; and upon our walls they should be left but like a ragged staff, not above two or three eyes at most upon the bearing branches; and the lower the vine and fewer the branches, the grapes will be still the better.

The best figure of a garden is either a square or an oblong, and either upon a flat or a descent; they have all their beauties, but the best I esteem an oblong upon a descent. The beauty, the air, the view makes amends for the expense, which is very great in finishing and supporting the terrace-walks, in levelling the parterres, and in the stone stairs that are necessary from one to the other.

The perfectest figure of a garden I ever saw, either at home or abroad, was that of Moor Park in Hertfordshire, when I knew it about thirty years ago. It was made by the Countess of Bedford, esteemed

among the greatest wits of her time, and celebrated by
Doctor Donne; and with very great care, excellent
contrivance, and much cost; but greater sums may be
thrown away without effect or honour, if there want
sense in proportion to money, or if Nature be not followed; which I take to be the great rule in this, and
perhaps in everything else, as far as the conduct not
only of our lives, but our governments. And whether
the greatest of mortal men should attempt the forcing
of Nature, may best be judged by observing how seldom God Almighty does it himself, by so few true and
undisputed miracles as we see or hear of in the world.
For my own part, I know not three wiser precepts for
the conduct either of princes or private men, than—

> —*Servare modum, finempue tueri,*
> *Naturamque sequi.*

Because I take the garden I have named to have been
in all kinds the most beautiful and perfect, at least in
the figure and disposition, that I have ever seen, I
will describe it for a model to those that meet with
such a situation, and are above the regards of common expense. It lies on the side of a hill (upon which
the house stands) but not very steep. The length of
the house, where the best rooms and of most use or
pleasure are, lies upon the breadth of the garden, the
great parlour opens into the middle of a terraced
gravel-walk that lies even with it, and which may be,

as I remember, about three hundred paces long, and broad in proportion; the border set with standard laurels, and at large distances, which have the beauty of orange trees out of flower and fruit: from this walk are three descents by many stone steps, in the middle and at each end, into a very large parterre. This is divided into quarters by gravel-walks, and adorned with two fountains and eight statues in the several quarters; at the end of the terrace-walk are two summer-houses, and the sides of the parterre are ranged with two large cloisters, open to the garden, upon arches of stone, and ending with two other summer-houses even with the cloisters, which are paved with stone, and designed for walks of shade, there being none other in the whole parterre. Over these two cloisters are two terraces covered with lead, and fenced with balusters; and the passage into these airy walks is out of the two summer-houses, at the end of the first ter-race-walk. The cloister facing the south is covered with vines, and would have been proper for an orange-house, and the other for myrtles, or other more common greens; and had, I doubt not, been cast for that purpose, if this piece of gardening had been then in as much vogue as it is now.

From the middle of the parterre is a descent by many steps flying on each side of a grotto that lies between them (covered with lead, and flat) into the lower garden, which is all fruit trees, ranged about the several quarters of a wilderness which is very shady; the walks here are all green, the grotto embellished with figures of shell-rockwork, fountains, and waterworks. If the hill had not ended with the lower garden, and the wall were not bounded by a common way that goes through the park, they might have added a third quarter of all greens; but this want is supplied by a garden on the other side the house, which is all of that sort, very wild, shady, and adorned with rough rockwork and fountains.

This was Moor Park when I was acquainted with it, and the sweetest place, I think, that I have seen in my life, either before or since, at home or abroad; what it is now, I can give little account, having passed through several hands that have made great changes in gardens as well as houses; but the remembrance of what it was is too pleasant ever to forget, and therefore I do not believe to have mistaken the figure of it, which may serve for a pattern to the best gardens of our manner, and that are most proper for our country and climate.

What I have said, of the best forms of gardens, is meant only of such as are in some sort regular; for there may be other forms wholly irregular that may, for aught I know, have more beauty than any of the others; but they must owe it to some extraordinary dispositions of nature in the seat, or some great race of fancy or judgement in the contrivance, which may reduce many disagreeing parts into some figure, which shall yet, upon the whole, be very agreeable.

Something of this I have seen in some places, but heard more of it from others who have lived much among the Chinese; a people, whose way of thinking seems to lie as wide of ours in Europe, as their country does. Among us, the beauty of building and planting is placed chiefly in some certain proportions, symmetries, or uniformities; our walks and our trees ranged so as to answer one another, and at exact distances. The Chinese scorn this way of planting, and say, a boy that can tell an hundred, may plant walks of trees in straight lines, and over against one another, and to what length and extent he pleases. But their greatest reach of imagination is employed in contriving figures, where the beauty shall be great, and strike the eye, but without any order or disposition of parts that shall be commonly or easily observed. And though we have hardly any notion of this sort of beauty, yet they have a particular word to express it; and where they find it hit their eye at first sight, they say the Sharawadgi is fine or is admirable, or any such expression of esteem. And whoever observes the work upon the best Indian gowns, or the painting upon their best screens or purcellans, will find their beauty is all of this kind (that is) without order. But I should hardly advise any of these attempts in the figure of gardens among us; they are adventures of too hard achievement for any common hands; and, though there may be more honour if they succeed well, yet there is more dishonour if they fail, and 'tis twenty to one they will; whereas, in regular figures, 'tis hard to make any great and remarkable faults.

The picture I have met with in some relations of a garden made by a Dutch governor of their colony, upon the Cape de Bonne Esperance, is admirable, and described to be an oblong figure, of very large extent, and divided into four quarters, by long and cross walks, ranged with all sorts of orange trees, lemons, limes, and citrons; each of these four quarters is planted with the trees, fruits, flowers, and plants that are native and proper to each of the four parts of the world; so as in this one enclosure are to be found the several gardens of Europe, Asia, Africa, and America. There could not be, in my mind, a greater thought of a gardener, nor a nobler idea of a garden, nor better suited or chosen for the climate, which is about thirty degrees, and may pass for the Hesperides of our age, whatever or wherever the other was. Yet this is agreed by all to have been in the islands or continent upon the south-west of Africa, but what their forms or their fruits were, none, that I know, pretend to tell; nor whether their golden apples were for taste, or only for sight, as those of Montezuma were in Mexico, who had large trees, with stocks, branches, leaves, and fruits, all admirably composed and wrought of gold; but this was only stupendous in cost and art, and answers not at all, in my opinion, the delicious varieties of Nature in other gardens.

What I have said of gardening is perhaps enough for any gentleman to know, so as to make no great faults, nor be much imposed upon in the designs of that kind, which I think ought to be applauded, and encouraged in all countries; that and building being a sort of creation, that raise beautiful fabrics and figures out of nothing, that make the convenience and pleasure of all private habitations, that employ many hands, and circulate much money among the poorer sort and artisans, that are a public service to one's country, by the example as well as effect, which adorn the scene, improve the earth, and even the air itself in some degree. The rest that belongs to this subject must be a gardener's part; upon whose skill, diligence, and care, the beauty of the grounds and excellence of the fruits will much depend. Though if the soil and sorts be well chosen, well suited, and disposed to the walls, the ignorance or carelessness of the servants can hardly leave the master disappointed.

I will not enter further upon his trade, than by three short directions or advice: first, in all plantations, either for his master or himself, to draw his trees out of some nursery that is upon a leaner and lighter soil than his own where he removes them; without this care they will not thrive in several years, perhaps never; and must make way for new, which should be avoided all that can be; for life is too short and uncertain to be renewing often your plantations. The walls of your garden, without their furniture, look as ill as those of your house; so that you cannot dig up your garden too often, nor too seldom cut them down.

The second is, in all trees you raise, to have some regard to the stock, as well as the graft or bud; for the first will have a share in giving taste and season to the fruits it produces, how little soever it is usually observed by our gardeners. I have found grafts of the same tree, upon a Bon-Cretien stock bring Chasseray pears that lasted till March, but with a rind green and rough: and others, upon a Metre-John stock, with a smooth and yellow skin, which were rotten in November. I am apt to think, all the difference between the St. Michael and the Ambrette pear (which has puzzled our gardeners) is only what comes from this variety of the stocks; and by this, perhaps, as well as by raising from stones and kernels, most of the new fruits are produced every age. So the grafting a crab upon a white thorn brings the Lazarolli, a fruit esteemed at Rome, though I do not find it worth cultivating here; and I believe the Cidrato (or Hermaphrodite) came from budding a citron upon an orange. The best peaches are raised by buds of the best fruits upon stocks growing from stones of the best peaches; and so the best apples and pears, from the best kinds grafted upon stocks from kernels also of the best sorts, with respect to the season, as well as beauty and taste. And I believe so many excellent winter pears, as have come into France since forty years, may have been found out by grafting summer pears of the finest taste and most water upon winter stocks.

The third advice is, to take the greatest care and pains in preserving your trees from the worst disease, to which those of the best fruits are subject in the best soils, and upon the best walls. 'Tis what has not been (that I know of) taken notice of with us, till I was forced to observe it by the experience of my gardens, though I have since met with it in books both ancient and modern. I found my vines, peaches, apricots, and plums upon my best south walls, and sometimes upon my west, apt for several years to a soot or smuttiness upon their leaves first, and then upon their fruits, which were good for nothing the years they were so affected. My orange trees were likewise subject to it, and never prospered while they were so; and I have known some collections quite destroyed by it. But I cannot say that I ever found either my figs or pears infected with it, nor any trees upon my east walls, though I do not well conjecture at the reason. The rest were so spoiled with it, that I complained to several of the oldest and best gardeners of England, who knew nothing of it, but that they often fell into the same misfortune, and esteemed it some blight of the spring. I observed after some years, that the diseased trees had very frequent upon their stocks and branches a small insect of a dark brown colour, figured like a shield, and about the size of a large wheat-corn: they stuck close to the bark, and in many places covered it, especially about the joints: in winter they are dry, and thin-shelled, but in spring they begin to grow soft, and to fill with moisture, and to throw a spawn like a black dust upon the stocks, as well as the leaves and fruits.

I met afterwards with the mention of this disease, as known among orange trees, in a book written upon that subject in Holland, and since in Pausanias, as a thing so much taken notice of in Greece, that the author describes a certain sort of earth which cures *Pediculos Vitis*, or, the lice of the vine. This is of all others the most pestilent disease of the best fruit trees, and upon the very best soils of gravel and sand (especially where they are too hungry): and is so contagious, that it is propagated to new plants raised from old trees that are infected, and spreads to new ones that are planted near them, which makes me imagine that it lies in the root, and that the best cure were by application there. But I have tried all sorts of soil without effect, and can prescribe no other remedy, than to prune your trees as close as you can, especially the tainted wood, then to wash them very clean with a wet brush, so as not to leave one shell upon them that you can discern: and upon our oranges to pick off every one that you can find by turning every leaf, as well as brushing clean the stocks and branches. Without these cares and diligences, you had better root up any trees that are infected, renew all the mould in your borders or boxes, and plant new sound trees, rather than suffer the disappointments and vexation of your old ones.

I may perhaps be allowed to know something of this trade, since I have so long allowed myself to be good for nothing else, which few men will do, or enjoy their gardens, without often looking abroad to see how other matters play, what motions in the State, and what invitations they may hope for into other scenes.

For my own part, as the country life, and this part of it more particularly, were the inclination of my youth itself, so they are the pleasure of my age; and I can truly say, that, among many great employments that have fallen to my share, I have never asked or sought for any one of them, but often endeavoured to escape from them, into the ease and freedom of a private scene, where a man may go his own way and his own pace, in the common paths or circles of life.

> *Inter cuncta leges et percunctabere doctos*
> *Qua ratione queas traducere leniter ævum,*
> *Quid curas minuat, quid te tibi reddat amicum,*
> *Quid pure tranquillet, honos, an dulce lucellum,*
> *An secretum iter, et fallentis semita vitæ.*

> But above all, the learned read and ask
> By what means you may gently pass your age,
> What lessens care, what makes thee thine own friend,
> What truly calms the mind; honour, or wealth,
> Or else a private path of stealing life?

These are questions that a man ought at least to ask

himself, whether he asks others or not, and to choose his course of life rather by his own humour and temper, than by common accidents, or advice of friends; at least if the Spanish proverb be true, that *a fool knows more in his own house, than a wise man in another's.*

The measure of choosing well is, whether a man likes what he has chosen, which I thank God has befallen me; and though among the follies of my life, building and planting have not been the least, and have cost me more than I have the confidence to own; yet they have been fully recompensed by the sweetness and satisfaction of this retreat, where, since my resolution taken of never entering again into any public employments, I have passed five years without ever going once to town, though I am almost in sight of it, and have a house there always ready to receive me. Nor has this been any sort of affectation, as some have thought it, but a mere want of desire or humour to make so small a remove; for when I am in this corner, I can truly say with Horace,

> *Me quoties reficit gelidus Digentia rivus,*
> *Quid sentire putas, quid credis amice precare?*
> *Sit mihi quod nunc est etiam minus, ut mihi vivam,*
> *Quod superest ævi, si quid superesse volent Dii.*
> *Sit bona librorum, et provisæ frugis in annum*
> *Copia, ne dubiæ fluitem spe pendulus horæ,*
> *Hoc satis est orasse Jovem, qui donat et aufert.*

Me when the cold Digentian stream revives,
What does my friend believe I think or ask?
Let me yet less possess, so I may live,
Whate'er of life remains, unto myself.
May I have books enough, and one year's store,
Not to depend upon each doubtful hour;
This is enough of mighty Jove to pray,
Who, as he pleases, gives and takes away.

That which makes the cares of gardening more necessary, or at least more excusable, is, that all men eat
fruit that can get it; so as the choice is only whether
one will eat good or ill; and between these the difference is not greater in point of taste and delicacy, than
it is of health: for the first I will only say, that whoever
has used to eat good will do very great penance when
he comes to ill: and for the other, I think nothing is
more evident, than as ill or unripe fruit is extremely
unwholesome, and causes so many untimely deaths,
or so much sickness about autumn, in all great cities
where 'tis greedily sold as well as eaten; so no part of
diet, in any season, is so healthful, so natural, and so
agreeable to the stomach as good and well-ripened
fruits; for this I make the measure of their being good:
and let the kinds be what they will, if they will not
ripen perfectly in our climate, they are better never
planted, or never eaten. I can say it for myself at
least, and all my friends, that the season of summer
fruits is ever the season of health with us, which I

reckon from the beginning of June to the end of
September: and for all sicknesses of the stomach
(from which most others are judged to proceed), I do
not think any that are, like me, the most subject to
them, shall complain, whenever they eat thirty or
forty cherries before meals, or the like proportion of
strawberries, white figs, soft peaches, or grapes perfectly ripe. But these after Michaelmas I do not think
wholesome with us, unless attended by some fit of hot
and dry weather; more than is usual after that season:
when the frosts or the rain hath taken them, they
grow dangerous, and nothing but the autumn and
winter pears are to be reckoned in season, besides
apples, which, with cherries, are of all others the most
innocent food, and perhaps the best physic. Now whoever will be sure to eat good fruit, must do it out of a
garden of his own; for, besides the choice so necessary
in the sorts, the soil, and so many other circumstances
that go to compose a good garden, and produce good
fruits, there is something very nice in gathering them,
and choosing the best, even from the same tree. The
best sorts of all among us, which I esteem the white
figs and the soft peaches, will not carry without suf-
fering. The best fruit that is bought, has no more of
the master's care, than how to raise the greatest gains;
his business is to have as much fruit as he can upon a
few trees; whereas the way to have it excellent is to
have but little upon many trees. So that for all things
out of a garden, either of salads or fruits, a poor man

will eat better, that has one of his own, than a rich man that has none. And this is all I think of necessary and useful to be known upon this subject.

First published 1685

This edition first published 2004 by
Pallas Editions
in conjunction with
Ostara Publishing

For more information about Pallas Editions
please write to
Pallas Athene (Publishers) Ltd.,
42 Spencer Rise
London NW5 1AP
or visit
www.pallasathene.co.uk

Series editors:
Alexander Fyjis-Walker
Andrew Cocks

Assistant editor: Gemma Davies

Cover photograph of the parterre at
Westbury Court Garden, Gloucestershire,
laid out 1696-1705,
National Trust Photographic Library/Ian Shaw.
Frontispiece portrait of Sir William Temple
engraved by George Vertue
after Sir Peter Lely

ISBN 1 873429 84 3

Printed in England